Ancestral Tree

Trent Busch

Cyberwit.net
HIG 45 Kaushambi Kunj, Kalindipuram
Allahabad - 211011 (U.P.) India
http://www.cyberwit.net
Tel: +(91) 9415091004
E-mail: info@cyberwit.net

Printed at Repro India Limited.

To Carol, Again

Acknowledgements

I would like to thank my granddaughter Peyton Busch Carper for helping me put this book together,

Faye Altman for her usual dead-on cover art, and Clint Nicely for his advice and encouragement over the last fifty years.

Acknowledgments

Thanks to the editors of the following publications where poems, sometimes with different titles and in different form, first appeared:

Agni Online, "The Forties"
American Journal of Nursing: "Clarence II"
The American Scholar: "I.T. Davis"
Anthology of Magazine Verse and Yearbook of Poetry, 1985, "Staying"
Antietam Review, "Ancestral"
Arts and Letters, "Curt's Girl"
Atelier of Healing, "Mother's Voices"
Atlanta Review, "Pleasant Hill School"
The Best American Poetry, 2001: "Heartland"
Blue Unicorn: "Miss Emily's Bun"
The Broome Review, "Nomenclature"
Carolina Quarterly, "Romey Davis"
Clackamas Literary Review, "Grandmother"
Clockwatch Review, "The Orchard"
Cold Mountain Review, "Lucy Snider"
The Chicago Review: "Reunion"
Cottonwood: "Uncle Chalmer's Wife"
Cottonwood Retrospective: "Uncle Chalmer's Wife"
Engaging Poetry: "I.T. Davis"
The Florida Review, "Back Road to Charleston"
Folio: "Karen Walking,
The Georgia Review: "Our Old German Grandmother"
Greensboro Review, "Treading Time"
Guesthouse, "Joe and Uncle Jesse"

Hawai'i Review: "The Whittler"
Hubbub, "Chasing Women"
The Hudson Review: "Aunt Ester and Uncle Jim," "Home Place," and "Sisters"
Interim, "Pupils of Discipline"
Jabberwock: "Aunt Alma"
Kansas Quarterly, "Late September Air"
Mankato Poetry Review, "The Garden"
Manoa: "Dora Ann,"
The Marlboro Review, "Three Sons"
Missing Spoke: "Uncle Arthur"
The Moving Force Journal, "But Its Own"
The Nation: "Heartland,"
Natural Bridge: "Uncle John Speaks of Dawn Mountain Fog"
New England Review, "The Country"
New York Quarterly: "For All the Miles,"

The Ohio Journal, "Mail Pouch Curry"
Owen Wister Review, "When I Touched your Arm"
Poetry: "Aletha," "Aunt Violet in a Swing," "Gay," and "Staying"
Puckerbrush Review, "Straight Creek"
Rockhurst Review: "Granddaughter Going West"
San Pedro River Review: "Kick Back"
Santa Fe Literary Review: Ed Stops by to Talk Philosophy"
Slant: "Grandfather Ghost"
So It Goes, The Literary Journal of the Kurt Vonnegut Museum
"Aunt Priscilla's Take on Viagra"
Subnivean, "Eulogy for Uncle Ben" and "Store"
The Tampa Review, "Sure Tones"
Thin Air Magazine, "Aunt Phyllis"
The Threepenny Review: "The Uncle"
Under a Warm Green Linden: "Grindstone"

Water-Stone Review, "Ancestral"
Writer's Forum, "Uncle Ace"
Zone 3: "Copperhead"

INTRODUCTION

The latest collection from Trent Busch, *Ancient Tree,* is one that burrows deeply into the underpinnings of what it means to be from a place, and a people and a culture. Like the characters which populate Willliam Faulkner's Yoknapatawpha, County, that very place being a character, the characters and places which appear in these poems are portrayed with heart and grit and sympathy but never judgment or blame or undue praise. Together they delineate the essence of Busch's native roots in rural central West Virginia during the later-mid twentieth century—a tough self-sufficient people in a land that is beautiful but challenging, and can be wholly unforgiving as well.

Employing the surnames of his four grandparents to portray the branches of his familial lineage, Busch encompasses five generations, concluding with his own family as they evolve into a new time and place and culture. If a picture is indeed "worth a thousand words," then the words herein create a multiple of pictures. It seems as if we are perhaps looking through an old family scrapbook, maybe a photo album, and relating the various pictures to people and events and places. And while most of the poems deal with particular people or places, they are universal in theme and concept such that we can see ourselves and perhaps our own friends and family members in them. These are good people, honest and hardworking, but also with flaws and vulnerabilities. Busch treats them openly and honestly as they wrestle with the ups and downs of love and loss and hope, maybe occasional regret and ultimately the determination to go on. They are in so many ways *"every family."*

Once again, with this his sixth collection, Busch demonstrate his master craftsmanship with crisp imagery and precise language. In this poetic biography of not only a people but also a place and a culture, Busch opens windows of memory through which we can recall our defeats and our failures, and hopefully the occasional successes as well. By probing the relationship between memory and truth, Busch allows, maybe challenges to consider the legacies and relationships of our own family trees: to mourn and miss the dead and dying branches, to cheer the sturdy limbs, and to celebrate the young new growth as well. These poems are hat poems should be; they examine people in the real experience of human life. They are funny and uplifting and tragic and sad and hopeful, and they hold up a mirror through which each of us might examine our own *Ancestral Tree.*

Clint Nicely

April, 2025

Contents

PROLOGUE

FAMILY HISTORY

Just behind the left temple
is a stairway that climbs
through a May afternoon
toward a damp bedroom
with a high bed.
Image
ends there. Now, on its own,
in motion, a young girl,
aging quickly, stands at
the window looking out.

Daughter, sister, mother,
the bed her wheelbarrow,
she pushes it before
her, our own grandmother.

From nowhere night began
and she carried her lamp
downstairs to a light switch
beside the kitchen door.

Just behind the left temple
is a May afternoon,
heads bow, hands join, children
glance up gravely into
the opened world.
Image
is gone. Its own, it leaves
us to redeem our deeds
and motors, whatever
beds we push before us.

1. Munday

AUNT HUGHIE

Seeing her sitting in a worn
coat on cold mornings, blowing
steam from her coffee, we watch
her stare out the window

at a hunched bird settled on
the light wire outside our
building, guessing her talent
when she was Miss State Fair:

did she in a tight sweater
sing an old Clooney song
or in shorts send high into
the air magic batons?

We watch and look away
and watch again, trying
to remember when she forgot
her days, when her interest

in questions dimmed, answers
dressed in buttoned collars, purse
missing when she went shopping,
gestures coming without hands.

Again, we watch, an aunt we
know by photographs now taken
from her, unable to coax from
memory what the pictures say.

STORE

If my parents died I'd come
and live with her I said,
all the while eyeing the candy
case, the box of balloons open
on the counter, clipped peanuts,

my parents ordering sugar,
flour, cornflakes, salt fish
in a barrel just delivered, how I
was too big in her arms,
her perfume, overprice of rouge.

It was about being her boy when
she told it, her overflowing
heart blowzed out with imagery,
my lowered eyes and quick grin
learned to hide embarrassment.

How strange we surely were
to those outside it, the colors
and smells and listings
combined in that selfishness
for sweetness that united us,

sharing lies with no meanness,
our purses lined at no expense
to others, her husband finding
me the years after she died to
say that he had lost his sweetheart.

CURT'S GIRL

A woman of passion surely,
Curt's girl; "I lost my sweetheart,"
he said, his shoulders bird round,
the grief so surprised on his face
it costly resembled a grin.

Rosa, Rosa, standing in the vines,
he her next husband, young
too young, she would wear him thin
fingers said, stopping on a dime
the tractor trailer, her hero.

Curt's girl, high cheekbones, running
her late husband's store too alone;
he second, hauling goods, strong arms,
cooking for his new one, rolling
barrels by night in her store room.

"I lost my sweetheart," forlorn, boom
goes the girl, the sometimes mother
slipping on the slick berm, the worm
urging its sting on the late bloom,
reclaimed by an afternoon wind.

Curt with his girl gone (his lost
sweetheart), ghost truck sloshing on
the creek road stones, the old pain soon,
transferred yonder by rain or moon
to flowers on the pale hillside

HEARTLAND

And she saying, I cannot quite
hear what she says, but he, standing
in clothes washed too often still
to be warm, looks out at the land.

And she saying, I cannot hear
what follows his name, and he, "What's
it all meant, Lizzie? We've made
a living and no one doubts our name."

And he remembering the years
before the green combines and long,
open barns for machinery
and their hands on each other young.

And she saying, I cannot tell
whether or not it's comforting,
until he turns to a door that
is not a new house and goes in.

And she saying, I can hear now,
"If the words are old, let them be.
It's hard enough with a dream;
here, what can you see of a plan?"

And he nodding, I can no longer
hear what she says, the house shadowed
by combines and long open barns,
the fields planted and bare for rain.

CLARENCE II

They say you have the big
C now, Clarence, you who
amazed us, tearing
down motors, building up
the ruptured parts, talking
and resting, dragging
deep that first-hand smoke.

How you bragged, Clarence, no
motor you couldn't fix,
and we, marveling, staying
half the night to listen
to it all, jacking you up,
telling everyone we knew.

They say you can't fix this
one, Clarence; they say
you are on your back in
another room where bearings
come only as shipments
in a dream, where now it
is you who must listen.

Christ, Clarence, hell, tell
us what throttles to pull;
how to trick the hoists to
lift, how to free the bolts;
don't lie there choking us

down, you who taught us no
engine was past repair.

They say you won't heed
reason, bruising knuckles,
accelerating, asking for
a thicker manual while
weeds block the windows of
your shop, enshrining your
smoke, remaining the one
place we once wanted to go.

THE WHITTLER

I always thought you were on verge
of genius, the way you whittled
kittens, sheep, old soldiers to stand
on our window sills as a breeze coaxed
us to dream of storefront Indians.

How could one with such power
on another day pare a pole
down to nothing but shavings, all
the time remaining silent while
loafers on porches ignored you?

Our motive for wishing you full
success was our lack: tops from spools
that wouldn't balance, homemade kites
we wore our soles out raising that,
once flying, remained in branches as
crosspiece decorations for Christmas.

Still I see you, fingering through
small boxes, pausing to drop
a figure in my hand, a dog,
perhaps, stopped in a rainy field
to shake itself, then, catching scent,
running off into mist again.

GRANDMOTHER

Helping with arguments
when he had to
Grandfather sat the porch
mostly,

shaving the tobacco plug,
chewing sparing
but regular.

He let Grandmother
do the work,
since she would,
Somebody has to,
Grandfather saying,
All right, Mother.

Because she always
stayed on the right
of things,
from saving the cow
not calf
when it breeched,
One milker is worth
three little bulls,
to correcting
the fourteen-cent mistake
on the store bill.

Except for once

when Grandfather
lost the big argument
she, Spare no cost,
bought the finest blue
coffin in the storeroom,

and standing beside him
on her own grave
finger down said,
That man all his life
walked, let him,
God grab his soul,
ride to Heaven
on golden wheels.

PUPILS OF DISCIPLINE

Out a ridge somewhere after the clay
road has forked, a stern man dressed
in a wrinkled shirt sits on a horse
and waits for us to catch up.

He is waiting to descend into
the valley of the other, where
corn has tasseled and now stands in
shocks, where summer has hidden.

Light through the branches of the baring
oaks makes his face a quiet cliff
but we know his impatience, our
speech slight as we hurry after.

Our young lives follow this leader
without contest or challenge, loaning
dissatisfaction for those who
idle in halls of the taken.

He pulls the rein, urges his horse
downward toward that strict valley
where only the damned or pupils
of discipline follow after.

AUNT ALMA

The house is a creaking
of drying boards. I have
lit the front room and bedroom
fires, the pilot light for
the water heater in
the closet off the kitchen.

Outside, snow has begun
to stick on the fringes
of the road and on the sides
of maple and locust trees.

Such a welcome home,
returning to a house
that would embrace me had
it arms, my sister says.

Comfort is knowing there
are no timbers waiting here
to fall, no ghosts in walls
to protect a former owner:

it knows me, like the old
dog Lawrence used to have
that growled any night he
came home late, but never
raised its head at me.

Death wears a soft shoe here,
and when I die will step
a waltz, sweeping me a
beauty from the ball to his
dark door, to a room where
I'll think I'll want to go.

MISS EMILY'S BUN

There is no having fun
in this life,
tight spooled, pinned,
barretted,
moving with the strict nose
of the library countenanced.

If I work loose enough
at mid-morning
to summon the glance
of a stranger
I am tucked and powdered
as if I were a child.

And by afternoon, many times
poked with pencils,
harassed by glasses,
I am stayed tighter
than a girdle on someone's
great-aunt Grundella.

Evenings out, it is
uptight all over again,
even if
the long-stemmed drinking
elicits only a shrug
for straying.

What joy is there spilled
alone on a chair?
I would talk to Cleopatra,
the blond on the corner.
Effete? No, a curl
in a world with no horrid.

REUNION

They are having a reunion
in the big house in the bottom.
No kin of mine, though old Johnson,
up the hollow yesterday checking
cattle, invited me to come.

I'll think about it, I said. What
family of mine would spit twice
to see my suitcase thrown before
me at their door. What family
either would I spit twice to see.

Five years I have slept this trailer,
living off the money of a war
I always hated, paid to the wife
of a missing soldier whom I
never loved. I did not ask for

justice, though I take it, the check
coming every month. If only
they could know the civilians that
I wasted in my night battles
soliciting impossible divorce.

That is done. Old Johnson asking
no questions, always proper, as
if it is my fidelity
that reunions are built on. This
morning I thought I might go down:

long tables built among the oaks
along the drive, heavy baskets
and checkered tablecloths, life or
death tag between the dusty cars,
men's cries and the ring of horseshoes.

Ten years since I got the letter.
What could I give there, what would they
give me? Woman in a trailer,
unrelated, alone, unwilling
to repent her ungratefulness.

AUNT PHYLLIS

No one thought of Aunt Phyllis
as anything more than a nosy
relative searching for night scraps.
She could take the smell straight
out of morning coffee, rumoring
red spots into breakfast
eggs, putting the cry back
into milk spilled, quitting
a world fast quitting her.

Then when worst was surely
over, she burst onto the end
of Christmas Eve, the button
and hole not matching on her
sweater, to say Grandmother
had once taken a hired man
as lover, so who knew which
of us might be a bastard or, just
as bad, sitting next to one.

If every life needs form, she
was the change that reels us
together when we stand outside
facing a north wind with
a burned-out house behind us,
or the change we need when
after months of evacuation, we
return to an overcast sky that
promises more desperate weather.

THE COUNTRY

The image must fit
the setting:
the hunter jumping
on the brush pile
must wear a red
and black mackinaw
with one button
missing; the rabbit
that breaks
for the fence line
must turn a somersault
when his shotgun
jerks upward
and springs tightly
against his shoulder.

The language must fit
the situation:
the girl who does not
want sex
with the boy with big
teeth must say,
"Shut your mouth, Jack,
and quit slobbering,"
or "Zip up, Lawrence,
if I get horny you'll
be the last to know."

Snow must have brown
grass rising through it,
pastures must have
small daisies,
cows must have dark
flies on their backs
and around their eyes.

When the sun rises
you will have already
thrown a bale
of hay from the loft
and stepped
in some horseshit.
When you come into
the kitchen
everyone will know
where you've been.

UNCLE ARTHUR

Well old uncle, old friend,
you have finally given
up the mind completely,
though you let it slip fast
these past two years, and have
taken the last of our
great family off, up
a final drive to the ridge.

The last time I wrote
about you was 1975
when you still took a drink
of whiskey and drove your
Plymouth down all roads,
getting lost for its
own sake, then using
directions for visits.

Farther back you made
moonshine in oak kegs, sold
it at dances where you
worked the music yourself,
playing your fiddle from
the shoulder rather than
the chin and dancing once
or twice with the ladies.

The question here is how
do I make you count

when you do not count,
as I do not count,
as even Socrates,
St. Augustine, Lincoln do
not count, only earth
separated from their names.

The last time I saw you,
you held a kitten you
had saved; you didn't know
my name. Today, rain pelts
the hayfield and the barn.
Were you back, you might tell
us what to say at this
end to an ancestral line.

2. DAVIS

ALETHA

Scythe on shoulder, Time
comes to cut the meadow,
heavy pipe in mouth, smoking
Five Brothers tobacco.

Popping daisies, laying
clover in swaths, he will
not be done until he
mows the timothy too.

How she stood in yellow
dress in the swale of spring
beeches, what kind of flower
pinned sideways in her hair.

Now he stands gaunt, tilting
blade against whetstone, guarding
the glass jug of water
he has hidden in the grass.

Dusk, he will be finished,
curved snath on shoulder, deep
in dark woods awaited by
the king's own carriage.

How she made them ashamed
of their advances, her
face trembling, her eyes shy
enough to quiet deer.

PLEASANT HILL SCHOOL

Out the ridge where the small
school used to stand, ruts of
water harbor tadpoles,
prosper beneath the trees.

From the soft breeze playing
in the branches, I try
to hear young voices loud
at tag or soft in watching,

or authoritative words
from our teacher, extolling
Roland's brave commitment
or merits of good spelling.

But I can only try,
for I have seen the ones
who moved to town, city
rounded or sick or dead

from cancer, and the ones
who stayed, gray upon their
heads, their eyes glassy with
age and remembrance.

And if there is singing
in these trees, it is for
the standing ruts filled with
water and bright nights when

the breeze rearranges
shadows, when young emerge
from frozen sleep and fill
the clearing with hoarse song.

POEM FOUND IN AN OLD TRUNK

The dog cocks his leg
against the maple
sapling, then trots
past the cellar and
goes out the gate
toward the orchard.

The sun is white
through the fog as
I harness the horses
to mow between
the apple trees.

I hear the mail truck
change gears as it climbs
toward the post office
in Beech Valley.

A morning rising in
light the same as any
other these seven years.

She has moved away.

ROMEY DAVIS

A bare tree stands against
the sky on a hilltop
a half mile from the house.
It is night and winter.
All afternoon it snowed,
but now the moon invites
night animals to come
from their dens and feed.
A star rises in the tree.

In the house a man is dead.
Relatives stoke the fire
and women talk quietly.
None say but would agree
the right amount of mourning
for one too old to live.

But night will miss this
man, who hunted foxes
and frightened owls, who set
steel traps in streams, who
reminded nature what it is.

He would not describe himself
this way, the star this way,
the moon, the snow, the tree.
He did not think that he
should die. No one views
a winter scene the same.

THE UNCLE

Work is not a comedy,
he said and rode the hay rake
into the fog, a road
we knew in our minds by heart

from traveling it
in the dark; we followed,
hearing hoofs and the ringing
of wheels upon the rocks.

If in that cave there was
any light—it took us years
to learn to laugh, to hold
a girl, to allow mistakes—

it was in the way we
learned to brush off bats, fear
no ghosts, adjust to damp,
be home in being lost.

Even so, he is here yet,
his heel upon the clutch,
releasing into the midday
sun those long rows that

took our sweat, if not our
hearts, and taught us hate
of levity that in that field
of hay was our success.

SISTERS

No one seemed to notice, or mind,
that she stayed on the fringe of things,
dangling her feet from a rock by
the river where we others swam,

only her sister understanding
her words, leading her up the slick
bank, helping with her shoes, brushing
leaves and mud from her legs and skirt.

School the same, standing far enough
from danger to avoid the bounding
ball, the uncontrollable, wild
bodies trampling the school yard.

Or question or imagine her thoughts
as she gazed at the honking geese,
then, after rain, stooped to return
earthworms from the sidewalk to the grass.

As if we knew we could not trip
the bolt if we dared, to lead her
across twilight to, for what was
us, the bright star of adulthood,

leaving it to her sister to
help her cross into her body's
center, teaching and learning herself
from the passage how not to fail.

FOR ALL THE MILES

How can we guess, knowing
little of their history,
what women of genius
felt in those days

when they looked out
at nightfall over their
husbands' fields, feeling
their bodies heavy with

another child, knowing
the absence of softness,
of tenderness the stern land
could not seed or allow?

how their youthful tears in
middle afternoons were
their only repose in
days filled with duty when

for all the miles theirs was
the single woman's voice
to soothe the outlaw wind?
until hearts took on what

cannot be written, strength
men dismiss as madness,
mouths lined with nothing
more to fear but the last

gift in a person's life,
like the she-wolf exiled
from the pack, voice high,
eyes closed against the moon.

UNCLE CHALMER'S WIFE

Another move, another borrowed
truck, boxing rags that were already
rags when we blew another breath
into another broken house.
Sweeping glass, cardboard tacked on missing
windowpanes, pretending the first
week that hammering can lean it straight.

Why do I stay with a man always
out of work, or when he finds a job,
sleeping in the first dark day of rain,
coming home the following noon
saying, "I can't work for that man."

I ask myself that question every
day. Always the fight, the make up.
Another job, then the wailing
walls and a ghost child on my hip.

I know what people say, what I
would say and probably did as
a small child growing up, about
the trash that loads their trash into
a borrowed pickup truck and moves
to a place already left as lost.

But now I stop and take one
final look, the kids hollering
and Chalmer yelling, "Hurry up."

Here and foolish, am I not allowed
to know what others know: that part
of me is taken there, that all
the world is older, that I stay
because of someplace else to go.

MAIL POUCH CURRY

His teeth are yellow.
Every day his sister
tells him to
clean up his mouth.

Once he did. Once
he brushed his teeth,
smiled at himself
in the looking glass,
and went to see
Ollie Anne Benson.

She let him kiss her.
He fell in love.
He put water on
his hair and took
her wild flowers.

She held onto his
arm. She told him
his bad habits.

She said tobacco breath
smelled like fox piss.
She said they
should get married.

He said he thought
they were. She said no.
He said he was late.

He likes his sister.
She cooks for him.
He says one woman
in a house is enough
to stay and keep
a mirror in her room.

AUNT PRISCILLA'S TAKE ON VIAGRA

You'd think God would let a man
rest and give a woman peace
after fifty years. Yet He's come
along (you feminists tell me now
He could be a woman) and dropped
a formula in some young (of course)
scientist's ear on how to raise
Mt. Richard from its limpid deep.

As if breakfast and underwear
and the weekly sweep were not enough,
now he's come squeezing and poking
his attention into every nook
a kitchen holds private, making
weekdays and chores already bad
worse with innuendoes about
weekend time trials and pole position.

I don't know what's to be done now
except to wish (you see the embarrassment
of prayer) that Nature, a woman herself,
somehow corrects the enormous
mistake by restoring to all of us
some intellect: why, from patriarch's
days it's been nothing but good sense
to leave the genitals blacked out.

I.T. DAVIS

Since I have time I will
tell you, Grandfather, that
the house is in decay,
road down, saplings trees.

I say since I have time
because over the years
you've kept me so busy
with the occurrences

of hills and woods, I've had
no life to catch you up.
Laura, the two-day-old
you rested on your knees

the night you died, is all
grown up as is her brother
whom you never met but has
your eyes and you would like.

They know some of your days,
but mostly not. Grandfather,
you taught me I must climb
in a world where others sat,

and, climbing, look neither
up nor back, the way maples
keep a close grip on the earth.
If I have done that, I

owe it to your advice,
yet must repeat the sad
news of your house and the road
you so expertly kept,

and remind you too, could
you come back, of a story
you often told about
the lumberjacks that you

*

marveled at when you were
just a boy, how it was
the ones who held on tight
who were the first to fall.

BUT ITS OWN

Over the ground I walk
on which he walked and now
lies under, I have walked
with my children and wife,
mother and grandmother,
father and grandfather.

A hill that overlooks
houses of those that all
hours might have stood in yards,
on porches, and seen where
they too, barring nothing,
would lie down separately.

The day is any day,
but its own, crows quiet
in the wooded hollows
once fields for the houses
with yards and porches, earth
in no way singular.

Seeds that blew, took root, bore
lie under wind above
the ground on which I walk,
over which he walked tall
as a poplar, too long
ago now for grieving.

UNCLE JOHN SPEAKS OF DAWN MOUNTAIN FOG

It starts off as a dot
no bigger than a bug
the size of a flea on
a landscape painting I
remember from London.

I want to nudge it with
a pencil tip to see
if it's moving when the scene
changes and it's moving
all right, a shadow

using flat rocks to cross
the creek, then following
a path that disappears
behind a bluff of grass
before emerging again,

more ghostly than shadow,
more saintly than ghost,
head leaning, legs straining,
climbing into clothing,
until dwarfing the morning

she appears on the steps,
undoing her scarf,
shaking mist from her hair,
smiling and, hand on hip,
saying, See, here I am.

LATE SEPTEMBER AIR

Up the bent walk to
the house door, stops
at the steps, smells
the dryness of fall in
the late September air.

Remembers something
as the breeze tousles
his hair and forgets
for a moment the key
in his hand.

Something a young girl
said, maybe, or a
woman standing, breaking
a sprig of lilac,
turning: eyes damp.

Who can know what
stops him, what holds
the key suspended in
his hand, his head
turned as if to listen.

As he would not say,
locked on that moment,
his face expressionless
to tell joy or grief,
tempered, far away.

SUMMER STORM

We have reached the time
of year of summer storms
and yesterday our cousin's
girl from down the road was
struck and killed by lightning.

The case was pictured
bold-faced in the paper
and we were shocked the more
by her large dog, seated
and panting beside her.

Drinking with two hands
we brace our morning
with black coffee and walk
from table to window
assessing our own yard.

Later, having gathered
and piled the broken limbs
in order, all will send
the usual cards that
rhyme our quiet sympathy.

Of course, it is the time
of year for storms, but now
all our family is
overwrought and moody:
the summer sky of last

night's lightning as white
as winter, and no one
to say for sure it was
but a summer birth,
with that sullen difference.

3 SNIDER

AUNT VIOLET IN A SWING

She dabs at her eyes,
sitting the porch swing,
and stares at the ridge
green-backed against
the sky.
She does not
know I watch, by chance
on a rise near the
garden, but I know
what has happened:

and who will fix the
faucet now when it
drips, drips long into
the night and replace
the burned-out light on

the cellar stairs? Who
will tramp with wet and
muddy feet and throw
carrots on the table?
Who will fix the lock?

Taken care of all her
life as if she were
a summer queen, her
audience is gone, the
forsaken garden dumb.

For this she weeps in
silence there and stares
at hills as young as
days when she still was
young, when
she loved a
man, when she would have
broken the rocky
field and slept on straw
had he but let her.

UNCLE ACE

Dead with the children,
though they are only dead
by distance, funeral visit away,
the heavy wife is lowered
beneath the blue canopy.

He will walk home, he says, not
far up the hollow to the ridge,
once their only road to town.
The daughters do not argue.

Home the eaves drip: clothes
to box for her sister;
mementos—the deal dresser
scattered with stick pins,
amber bottles, earrings and beads
he moved fifty years around
that will not adjust to his hands—
to put into a trunk and store away.

He touches the striped-back chair,
sees in the mirror the quilted
bed and clock, curses lowly
as hard thoughts skirt his brain,
threatening like horned angels:

a woman never pretty, just available,
a vessel for the throbbings
of an average man; how many nights

did he watch her flannelled back
until his own hungers died?

a woman with a barking voice,
whose shapeless presence
made him glad to eat alone,
whose ferret hands searched out
his whiskey, breaking bottles
against the corner stones
until he gave up drinking too;

a sick woman who would not die,
who ate the syrups, drank the pills,
lay the bed, weeping he did
not care for her and never was
the husband other women had.

But the angels only flirt. He has
knocked one like a wasp against
her picture with the two daughters.
Outside, night settles on the silent
house, eaves fill with darkened
water, the winter rain sets in.

THE FORTIES

In small towns in the forties
cats did not indulge mice;
they entertained themselves,

and Bill Snider drove his
dad's green Buick out dirt
roads, dusting the peach trees.

There were the usual dry
vines spit from anxious mouths
while the wild hay tasseled.

At stores, while supper fried,
white sacks flowered and hands
slapped their knees by dusk light.

Porcelain chinked as heat
blew the curtains, and mud
sucked the water from snow.

Outside, inside, these were
the small presents that kept
the lean and hungry hard

for the nothing past daylight
that would soften and ripen
and explode on the young.

KAREN WALKING

The girl in blue smock walks
at daybreak below stout
trees on the asphalt road.

She does not whistle, nor
talk to herself, eyes straight,
arms swinging fluidly.

She has awakened dogs
and startled the roosting
birds in the thick branches.

She knows but would not say
what else she will startle;
today she goes to the store.

Her grandmother walked this
road before her mother.
She will meet no strangers.

No one walks with her on
the asphalt road, her list
tucked into her blue smock.

She walks straight and her brown
shoes are comfortable;
she does not fear the dogs.

She understands the quietness
of the road, the long shadows
below the thick branches.

She knows and walks directly:
the sun is not yet hot
and she is in no hurry.

DORA ANN

A wild ringing in the summer
air, the road turns and turns; Uncle
Jim is dead, Madge Burch grows larger
and larger. The fit is on Jean.

False steps as the child holds the doll
closer; no one can say the word
to stop her rocking and staring
as the walls fly past the window.

Take her limp hand, it does no good;
touch her forehead, it is normal.
Send her brother to the store for
potatoes. Will she go with him?

"I want to go home." "But you are
home, dear." "I want to go home."
"Keep her from the news," Aunt Irma
says. "Events are stuffing her head."

At last something sane. "Where then is
home, my darling?" A butterfly
on the wild iris. Rocked in the lap
of the rabbit's apron, without dream.

She does not stop, she will never
stop. She feels no hunger, threat of
danger, no desire or anger,
no prompting at her mother's grief.

THREE SONS

I
Sun gleams off the tombstones
on the ridge, May sunny
morning and the smooth to
touch gray marble gleaming
and all inscriptions clear.

The crow over the ridge
flying, bright sun gleaming
off his hard wings, calling,
his cry muffled as he
sails down the deep hollow.

II
Where feet pass on the wooden floor
voices are low, talk in the hall
low, someone elbowing the door,
careful, not letting the wood fall.

In the kitchen women in Greek
chorus, dressed in shawls, tell a ride
said first by Lorca, wash the cheek
of both mother and virgin bride.

III
When I was young, I thought
sons lasted forever,
coming in with shirts and
pride torn, capacity

none whatsoever to
understand how when I
reached out my hand I was
waiting only for them
to get wiser, older.

To whom can I give the
impossible answer
when questioned, "What happens
to a mother's heart when
she loses all her sons?"
when I in that instant
see my own powdered face
lying lined and rigid,
them beside me weeping?

IV
They are adding another room
to the house. Workers this morning
with level and square, pine lumber.
They do a good job, and it is
something my husband has wanted.

The money comes from my oldest,
Gerald, who was killed in the war.
Would have been thirty-four today.
Always the dreamiest. Most people
say he looked like his father.

V
Night came and the last boy
was in the ground and I
thought, Dear God, what else have

you planned for this my one
life before it is done.

Her not crying anymore
and the neighbors gone and
when I saw my face in
the window I looked down
but could not see the floor.

VI
The rabbit stretches long before
the fox at dusk, then is caught at
the cemetery gate. Dead, it
is carried gently as a kitten.

The darkened ridge and crows calm as
a house dog barks in the hollow.
Monuments take form, and under
the quick moon cast shadows like men.

AUNT ESTHER AND UNCLE JIM

For a week now he has
not started his truck, back
and forth in a cold month
from barn to house, causing
her to say he might at
least go to the store and loaf.

There is no word again
today and as they sit
they wonder if what
the correspondent on
TV said was true: some
do not want to come back.

Her cousin's boy had been
killed outright and when they
brought the flagged box
into the church she got no
farther in her thoughts than
the shine on the soldier's boots.

She thought now about her
own boy's shoes and how each
morning after breakfast
and before the bus, he
shined them between his knees
and held them to the light.

She cannot remember
what she wanted for him then
or if she can she has
put it with old pieces
she used to save for quilts
on some forgotten shelf.

And what Jim thought, well
what man wasn't he like,
switching stations on and off
and talking gruff, wondering
if what the missing wished
is what those wishing do.

LUCY SNIDER

She ran into the forest,
white arms, white legs,
up hollows, across knobs,
the trees wailing.

She became a man with
a spike driven through
his eye. She held
her face, stumbling,
tripping over logs.

She became a woman
with a hatchet buried
in her skull. She
clutched at the handle,
leaping down a cliff,
running up a stream.

When she reached a
dark pool she tried
to scrub the white
from her arms and legs
but it spread to her
breasts and thighs.

She screamed, then went
under, thrashing
against a man's hands
penning her in a car.

Rangers wrapped her in
a blanket, parents
buried her on a ridge,
and a white rain washed
small gullies in the
clay of the red hills.

COPPERHEAD

Down the path from the road
I come walking. Past the
barn toward the back door
of the house.
It is daylight,
and I have bunched my dress
for an hour now, my legs
wet from the night grass.

I have been bitten by
a snake, thick, copper-headed,
the wound swelling and my
flesh a dizzy pink.

Who cares what kind, the snake,
who cares who, the coil more
frightening than the strike,
a sip of venom

from a tall glass, a thrown
away doll I wanted
only yesterday. Just
these last steps,
the stairs to
reach, then past the burning
lamp in my mama's face
and I will not die.

CHASING WOMEN

A beer between his knees, he slid
the car around turns with one hand,
the steering wheel knob a ruby
gliding in its socket, his hair
damp on the back of his neck.

Oh, we were after *women*, he
eighteen, I two years younger,
talking loud, dazzling
the countryside with speed
and liquor, the moment everything.

So when we asked them to join us,
we were not really struck by their
indifference; we had only time
to ease the needing heart for what
it needed, satisfied we could.

ED STOPS BY TO TALK PHILOSOPHY

"The tool you order is
never the same in person:
take this wrench here, as
advertised on TV
able to loosen the hind
quarter of a moose, a limp,
pussy-levered fidget
that couldn't jack the nuts
off a sixty-seven Buick;

"just as the person you
get is never the same tool,
whoever he or she
happens to be—I name
no one in particular,
say Lucille Ball, maybe,
or W.H. Auden, huddled
up little round backs with
dip-snuff mouths in a bar."

Now wait a minute, I look
at him, W.H. Auden?

"Hey, man, never think I
don't read my novels;
or that big-boobed Lara
game on the new Playstation:
I'd like to see her climb
up on my roof without

getting anything dirty,
then try to save poor old
Le Breun when he's loaded."

You got me there, I say.
"And a crescent can't be
a monkey wrench like on
that *Parasite Eve*—
but I see I'm losing you here;
the point being, that which
you make must be useful.

Sometimes, friends got to
drop by friends to keep
them on top of reality."

I'm much obliged, I say.

"You don't, it won't set fields
on fire; by example, I'm losing
this wrench faster than a gnat
can lick its ass and remember,
as always, you need me, whistle."

JOE AND UNCLE JESSE

"I quit," he said,
"just quit.
Happen you find
enough air
left in the tires
of that old '67 Plymouth,
have her!
But I'm through."

What else he said
I'm damned
if I remember;
he just stepped
off the store porch,
walked a half-mile
down the road
to Haverstraw's,
beat the whole field
at shuffle board,
and laid down and died.
In style, by God.

STRAIGHT CREEK

They have taken the bell
from the steeple and hung
it from a yoke between
two posts before the church.

The hillside field beside
it where horses galloped
once and boys caught and rode
them belongs to the night.

Though the air is dry and leaves
come down in bursts, it is
still summer, the long drought
unaffected by the small rain.

What the church meant beyond
its symbol to this town
I don't know, though I too
leaned my head in its pews

once and listened to the rough
words of elders, studying
the calligraphy in
hymnals and Betty Brown.

I do not know what it
is I could not learn, what
if it ever drifted down
passed through my hands like wind.

The bell is out of the steeple
now. Palpable as that bell,
surely, to them, cleansing
as the smile of Betty Brown.

KICK BACK

The day the triangle of wood
kicked off the saw blade through the screen
into the yard, Uncle Wenn had
just turned the corner of the shop.

It wasn't really Uncle Wenn,
of course, but you know how there is
always someone in the family
everyone hates to see coming,

usually just after you've bobbed
the tail off the cat or goddamned
some item that was behaving
in a way peculiar to your plan.

You who know can fill in what he
said and how long he took to say
it and what guilt he practically
never left behind when he went on.

Anyway, Uncle Wenn was gone
and I was left with a miter
ruined and half a day wasted,
another half needed for the screen,

which I notice this morning I
never got around to, frayed and dusty
so long no one asks about it
now, taking on years and the fate of

the words of Uncle Fake Uncle Wenn.
I suppose he exampled us
all once or another, never
guessing the bad we thought he was

doing goodness, cracked in his song,
as if one kick back through a screen
couldn't teach in a second the danger
of a thousand safely cut off ends.

EULOGY FOR UNCLE CHARLEY

Looking back on it, he did not
know what he might have changed,
the usual accidents bringing
him here to the ordinary.

There were roses to be grown so
he grew them, there was dirt
to be moved so he moved it:
not just talking but getting done.

And if surely done himself, still
focused, the tree line outside
the window marching up the rising
field like soldiers disappearing.

Looking back on it, he saw the wind
taking him a direction
he would not go in repetition,
nor repeating go that way again.

Trees climbed the field, wind took the seeds
to ground that would accept them. Let
that change, how they faded into
the land be his memorial.

4 BUSCH

THE ORCHARD

Peaches have had their fling;
now is the time apples
ripen, and bent limbs of
pears burden the orchard.

My father, nearly blind,
standing by the window
shows us the scrape on his hand
and wants to know why skin
in old age gets rotten.

Mother says that that is
no way for him to talk
in the kitchen and hands
him a bucket to get
some fruit for breakfast.

She says he has begun
to talk that way lately,
which was never like him,
and his children should
visit him more often.

I go outside to help,
though I am not needed,
the day fair as all of
them seem to be when I

remember: the crates,
the market, the dark hair
on my father's arms as
he secured the ladders.

What should we say to each
other? He is that man
no longer? I am not
the boy on his shoulders
stretching for the highest fruit?

Now workers tend the trees.
We both know I could have
stayed if I had wanted,
his urging me to town
a guise for stubbornness.

The sun blooms full, making
boughs shadow each other,
the pear trees like heavy
mothers, as my father,
hidden, takes their fruit,
gentle with the shaking limbs.

NOMENCLATURE

The trouble with my dad
and me was nomenclature:
he'd ask for a Crescent
and I'd bring a box end
forever the wrong size;

he'd ask for a hole saw,
I'd bring a drill bit,
ball-peen, a tack hammer;
a saw horse, I'd dream
a ticket to the fair.

Searching, I could out-swear
him, kicking the useless
toolbox aside, muttering
with the worst of him about
a quick road out of town.

Now it's similes for
metaphors, synecdoche
for metonymy, images
that show by the dead tree
there're no pears left to prize.

He made a wagon for us
once. Here, he said and went
inside. It rode all right.
All I wanted, one time, was
wasted breath, one tired lie.

HOME PLACE

They claim the house where I was born
their home place and own it still, our
father selling it, moving to
town our widowed neighbor said, though
the ones who lived there, including
her, made up not a hundred names.

Even if less and less I live there
still—the sudden foggy mornings
when cattle move like ghosts around
the barn, the beetled afternoons—
they have the deed to rearrange
any memories as their own.

When we played together, they could
have it free since any toy given
away was still our own, a whim
that but a moment might reverse,
as the oak might reclaim in spring
the dazzle it had given to the fall.

Can two or even more families
have one home? It was not new when
we moved in. Perhaps memories
are best kept by the house itself
loaning us its boards and land to
hoard our secrets, earning our
courtesy which we in turn give them.

GRANDFATHER GHOST

Out of summer heat
he comes with the odor
of broken earth woven
into his shirt,

sweat darkened front,
pants slack, shoes dark,
the back of his hands
crumbed with dirt.

Comes out of the dance of
summer heat to stand
in the barn's shadow,
browed eyes direct.

What have you come to tell
this time, old man, with
rough speech, cold advice,
gone kindness? Again

to say everything by
speaking of carrots, ways
to cure hay, the right
time of moon to cut hogs?

Old ghost, for God's
sake, old man, say what I
was to you, you in me, what
difference did we make?

Out of the shadow, he
returns to the dance of
summer heat, his shirt
still dark, his step

straight away from ways to
follow, toward lands where
praise is a dusty word
for which there is no call.

GRINDSTONE

The sun is out today,
bringing with its false hope
cold weather; on beaches
somewhere nearly naked
girls are turning themselves,
perhaps under umbrellas.

I'm not glad to be here
but not unglad not to
be there either, working
inside at something not
burdened with particulars
that I'll miter later.

Against the wall below
a window is a grindstone
once worked by my grandfather,
over which I have built
a small table; you can
see the handle I turned

for him hot summer days,
splash of rusty water,
wooden, right angled like
a bicycle pedal,
stuff on top of stuff with
stuff balanced above it.

They are putting lotion
on themselves on those beaches,
round and round in the sun.
Don't you ever tire of work?
I do not say, his hair
full, gray above the blade.

OUR OLD GERMAN GRANDMOTHER

Our old German grandmother
bombed out of Hamburg, asked,
"Are you religious?" answers,
stern across the cheek bones,
"My lineage, my name, my house
it is boomed, poof! The father
of my six children is five
years in Siberia—comes home
broken to die in my arms.
My children they starve. And should
I go to my knees for food?
No Jesus bread man gives outside
my door. What good miracles?
With these two hands I feed.
I raise them right. They make
me no trouble. I teach them good
from bad. No stealing. No cursing
in my house. They have the respect,
the pride. No, I do not believe."

MOTHER'S VOICES

Yesterday there was a voice;
today there is none. That's the way
it is when you lose the sound of
someone who's been always in your ear.

You heard the ring and you took it,
all those years of distinguishing
one tone from another, then
filtering out the hurt not meant

to last longer than the moment;
the it's all right you said later,
the tear that came too easily
dried after years of subtle wear.

It will not awake for breakfast
to say the sun they promised might
just come today, hoping eaves held
until that fellow came to fix them.

Today is sunny; sound carries well
out of the west where a breeze brings
the soft talk of neighbors telling
the postponement of pressing repair.

But voice is not there—the way
it told the clock, the obits in
the paper, the natural way
it broke between dishes and hands.

SURE TONES

We yell at the old ones
and when they don't understand
they pretend, holding
conversations with ghosts,

giving impossible answers,
changing the topic to
two years ago last winter
when the subject is zinnias.

At first we yell louder
but then unsettled by
the oh in their voices
our impatience causes,

we grow suspect of sound.
What we wish for most is
not their hearing back; they
can have that, even if

they never get quite used
to the batteries, whistling
soccer games in their head.
No, what we want back is

the Sunday afternoons
when they yelled at us at
the falls, the dog we could
not have, tones that were sure.

Lost now, we sit on porches
with them trying to make
them hear, trying to hear
ourselves not just those gone

voices but the perfect
blend that is not denial
or telling, that music
by which we speak and hear.

WHEN I TOUCHED YOUR ARM

Your cry in the night was
not the cry of death—
only, perhaps, the fear
of hurt for your child

or cry for some long ago
love who, standing on
your front steps, looking at
his hands as if he

held a hat, said he was
not coming back, feeling
again the pain in his
voice and then your pain.

When I touched your arm, I
felt the calmness return
as it did to Juliet
learning that mere Tybalt

was slain, yet crying
out again when she found
Romeo gone. I had
tried to return calm,

as one who offers
a balloon to a child
whose kite's string is all
that's left in her hand.

What made me think then
that kindness and guilt
are one, the child repulsed
by solution, your cry

growing, as if my hand,
not arrived in time,
signaled some wrong I had
made, some dark I had done?

BACK ROAD TO CHARLESTON

The calf, probably six
months old, stands at the edge
of the road ready to bolt.
I slow the car willing
to follow any lead,

then pass slowly, watching
it wobble in glass to
the center line and stand
again, seeing what calves
see, failed in direction.

I top the slow hill full
of options: try to find
its owner, find someone
who might find its owner,
get out and flag others.

And then, like God, do none
of these things, my wife's plane
due in Charleston,
morning sky suddenly
dark with our own dangers.

How right it would be to
have answers, smile down on
all highways and runways,
sure, shifting on without
the guilt of excuses.

I try the radio for
weather, static snapping,
and see the calf in the rain
that is coming, raising
its head, dripping, bawling.

TREADING TIME

for Kendall

Where the hickories have
been cut for the new road
we gather firewood. We
remember the old way.

The gas line runs under
the meter house and we
watch the many needles,
fast, slow, some not moving.

The wind in the old oaks
takes us away from each
other and you, staring,
see things I never saw.

And I see trees empty
of their leaves, at first cold,
December, then spring when
buds begin to sharpen.

You tell me that the drought
this year brought no mast
for the animals; you say
that that is nothing new.

We throw the wood over
the fender of the truck

and I notice the gray
beginning in your hair.

At the house you bring Scotch
in a brandy glass. You say
your daughter just finished
college. I say, mine too.

THE GARDEN

In a tin shed my brother
puts out a battery-run
radio to keep deer
out of his sweet corn.

We walk down to the garden
at night and listen
to the hidden ghosts
singing to each other.

Though the voices seem
lower when we return
the next morning,
they surprise us still.

Raccoons have ravaged
the field: leaves shredded,
tassels broken, the white
of canvas gloves.

Well, that worked,
he says, switching off
the radio, tearing
foil from the antenna.

We parade down rows, looking
at the half-eaten ears,
obscenities flying from
his mouth like ticker tape.

I thought those damned
things were extinct,
he says, not meaning it,
kicking at clods.

Then, looking away from
each other, past animals,
the blue hills, we laugh like
brothers, like West Virginians.

MACFARLAN BRIDGE

The Macfarlan bridge is
down, cables cut, wooden
floor and rusty girders
hauled away in trucks.

The sides of the new bridge,
cement white, no steel rod
showing, rise and block
the view of the river.

As a child, asleep at
night behind my father's
driving, I woke to boards
rattling, the signal

that the trip from town was
over. Later, cousins
and I walked to the river
and climbed, against parents'

wishes, the taut wires
to the top braces. No one
thought of falling then,
and no one did, for water

was a flowing away
from grown-up things to birds
that flew and could not fall
or fish that never drowned.

It is the permanence
of this bridge now, as I
stop today and look over:
no careless swaying, the dark

water claiming, drawing
my weight forward until
in panic I push away
and turn against falling.

In my car I drive away
trembling, that man back there,
gaunt, consenting, adult
in his body-breaking fall.

GAY

When you hold his hand
I try to understand
by thinking of
heterosexual love,

her hand in mine,
say, or watching highway
and mountains through
the windshield all day long,

suddenly turning
and catching her watching
face that, once caught,
smiles, wanting nothing else.

I do not know
if I am close; I don't
know what to ask,
how not to be embarrassed.

Asking, father
to his son, I know that,
a son myself,
words are bricks in your mouth

and offer this:
Is a date the way I felt
in high school asking
Vicki to the dance?

to be stood up,
the way I feel here, not
knowing what I've
done wrong or what I lack,

yet wanting still
another chance to prove
I am worthy
of trust and confidence?

Tonight in our
secret worlds I strive to
learn something right,
to be the man behind

you when you're dressed,
to help you with your ties,
to let you live
with love I cannot know.

STAYING

The house a party of motion,
camp, college, marriage—all the same:
something in a drawer almost
left behind, the double-checked closet.

No time yet for sidelong glances
or hang-down eyes, bodies scuffling,
a sudden cry at not much time,
flush of toilet, trunk lid slammed.

Standing like two birds we watch the
car back out the drive, a fluttering
hand between boxes that tilt, then
jostle and settle for the ride.

Daughter, daughter, have we prepared
you half so well for days ahead,
when clothes, lockets are forgotten,
when dark days and nights greet you with

surprises not taught here, and you
find a woman inside leaving
behind the girl you thought you were
because we thought you were that girl?

Like two birds we return to the branch
of our own lives, wondering if
we are lucky not to be true birds,
perched above nests emptied every year.

GRANDDAUGHTER GOING WEST

She unlocks the car door with no key,
the new-fashioned way, throws her coat
in back, puts her purse on the floor
of the front seat, and drives away.

No one's with her now, as surely
someone would have been a generation
earlier, as she set forth to cross
a country of what would then have

been mostly ordinary people
shocked at her bare leg on the top
step of a station where she'd pause for
rest and gas and Coca Cola.

Now she wears jeans on highways much
more hostile, the one behind her
not the first she's had to drive away
from to get over, nor the worst.

Before she's gone there will be many
fields of grain to wave, many signs
that will color the drab outskirts of
towns she'll both ignore and sleep in.

For just beyond the hood are lines
drawn that she guns over, erasing
doubt, guilt, taboos, and baggage, in
the old tradition, going west.

EPITHALAMIUM

The quilt rack I'm building
for my nephew was commissioned
in a silent deal: I'll make
you one on the promise
I'm spared the ceremony.

He made no promise, nor
was asked for one outside
the conversation I
tied the ribbon on of
present without presence.

How could he? Those other
ones who see the moment
of their lives beyond the whims
of sickness, golf, or I'd
rather be in Georgia.

It's three-quarters finished,
the arches a ring of
laminated oak,
dowels, stretchers, and base
a half year in the planning

to remind them on their June
day of Christmases
and the hard snowy nights
shared by their ancestors
in new, west Virginia.

In my mind, except for
flowers, I've played their song,
done the dance and built my
part of the bargain. Where they'll
get the quilt I do not know.

EPILOGUE

ANCESTRAL

Memory is never true. More
like a dream, the way we put
the extras in to round it out,
to give it story, to show the ones
we're telling to we may be worthy.

They know the lie, want it, so when
their turn comes round they can lean back
in demivolting fury or else
close in, shoulders together, to make
us sigh or yes our heads or stare.

It is the fiction now that pays,
the link that takes us back to the need
for warmth in groups, men's need for women,
women's need for men, women's
for women, the child's need for age.

Even if it is more true when we're
alone, when we drop the stone to
the bottom of the lake and go
diving there among light and shadows
for icons we need to right our lives,

it is still fancy. Yet it costs
us nothing, taking us near the ones
and things that are gone from our lives
forever save for this law that can
be broken, this gift from those lost times.